MANTIC

Mantic

by
Maureen Alsop

Augury Books
New York, New York

Copyright 2013 © Maureen Alsop
All rights reserved

Published in the United States of America
First Edition

Cover Image: "When I Close My Eyes" by Tasha Marie
Reproduced courtesy of Vesper Magazine
Book Design by Daniel Estrella
ISBN: 978-0-9887355-1-4

For reproduction inquiries or other information, please visit our website at:
www.augurybooks.com

Acknowledgements

The Antigonish Review, "Oromancy While Waiting for the Beloved," "Arundo Road"
Apt, "Alphitomancy"
Aperçus Quarterly, "Sambucus Road," "Hanael's Mandala of Water, Grass, Sun"
Action Yes, "The Guardian's Accurate Shotgun Upon Your Brow"
AGNI, "Epiphany"
Arsenic Lobster, "Catoptromancy"
Blackbird, "Moth, Horse, Accident, Skin"
Chaparral, "Phyllorhodomancy"
Copper Nickel, "Aureola"
diode, "The Arrival Memory," "Spring Tattoo,"
Escape Into Life, "Cledonomancy, Sleep in the Raven's Throat"
Georgetown Review, "Macharomancy"
Handsome, "Fugitive"
Harpur Palate, "Accidental Sea"
Interpoezia, "Spring"
Kestrel, "Radiesthesia," "Magastromancy"
Kenyon Review, "Ornithomancy," "Necromancy," "Eromancy"
Mental Shoes, "Ostentaria"
MiPOesias, "The Widowhood of Charlotte Keese"
New Delta Review, "Absentia," "Ensign March"
The Offending Adam, "Ilex Road," "Betula Road," "Hamamelis Road," "Hedera Road"
qarrtsiluni, "Ouranomancy," "Thumomancy"
Tampa Review, "Seaamong Sea"
Thrush, "Floromancy"
Tuesday; An Art Project, "Sideromancy"
Typo, "Bequest," "In Release of the Coming Passage," "Notes from the Blue Terrace," "Epithalamium"
Pank, "Gyromancy," "Enoptromancy," "Sciomancy"
Swink, "Dendromancy"
Versal, "Frost Altar"
Yew Journal, "Belief," "Hyomancy"

Several poems also appeared in *Narwhal* (Cannibal Books) as a chapbook, *Luminal Equation*. Additional poems appeared in the following chapbooks: *the dream and the dream you spoke* (Spire Press) and *Twelve Greatest Hits* (Pudding House Press).

"Belomancy" appeared in *Don't Blame the Ugly Mug Poetry Anthology* "Belomancy," and "Apantomancy" appeared in the anthology [*out of nothing*] #0: "theoretical perspectives on the substance preceding [nothing]."

"Cledonomancy, Sleep in the Raven's Throat" also appeared in the anthology *Bird As Black As the Sun* and in *Gallerie, A Journal of Ideas*.

for Steve

Gyromancy	17
Epiphany	18
Ouranomancy	19
Radiesthesia	20
Bequest	21
Belief	22
Notes from the Blue Terrace	23
Ornithomancy	24
The Guardian's Accurate Shotgun Upon Your Brow	25
Dendromancy, Ex Nihilo Nihil Fit	26
In Release of The Coming Passage	27
Catoptromancy	28
Moth, Horse, Accident, Skin	29
Hyomancy	30
The Arrival Memory	31
Thumomancy	32
Epithalamium	33
Alphitomancy	34
Fugitive	35
Accidental Sea	36
Necromancy	37
Aureola	38
Phyllorhodomancy	39
Seaamong Sea	40
Cledonomancy, Sleep in the Raven's Throat	41
Absentia	42
Sciomancy	43
Floromancy	44
Ensign March	45
The Widowhood of Charlotte Keese	46
Spring	47
Belomancy	48
Rhapsodomancy for an Imperfect Forecast	49
Oromancy While Waiting for the Beloved	52
Eromancy	59
Spring Tattoo	60
Ostentaria	61
Macharomancy	62
Hanael's Mandala of Water, Grass, Sun	63
Magastromancy	64
Sideromancy	65
Apantomancy	66
Enoptromancy	67
Frost Altar	68

Mantic

GYROMANCY
> *divination by walking around a circle of letters until dizzy you fall down on the letters or in the direction to take*

So you go wither. So muscled in foxglove. So the surface of passionflower's scent known to the lungs will be touched by the mouth. So a camera's song leans over the guardrail. So the graffiti of circles. So lexicon is devoured by chalk in the grassland. So omega. So bilge. So yesterday the tradition of order was left to the entangled hawfinch. So I refused. So I am not a lady. Not your supper jug. Your hunt of her. So dumpling, who's your fried chicken? Even in neon-fragment. Even in mastic-erotic-red. Your taste of me dispensed. So inconsolable keystrokes do not withdraw from honesty, as honesty is in itself inconsolable.

So found I was without you. I do not remember how you left. Transparent, history steeped in your head. So I held my finger to the small blossoms of your eyelids. So I told the sun to go. And there it spread. So flagstone. So eaglet.

Epiphany

The moment your body deserted the soul a last
spasm of air passed through your right
nostril. I will tell you

how it happened. Without
mercy & too
late you had learned that you were made
to be loved. Someone soaked your

nakedness in honey & oiled
your chest with pycnantha. Your head
was shaved. The red dark
room was lit by a single votive, & the draft from hallway
coaxed the flame
to dance. Your voice
rose pointless as no one
could hear you
muttering you still
thought you remembered
and insisted on it. You said *I remember stalling
over the wide white bed they say*

it is this love. In readiness, the radio
failed. A blueprint of static clamped
over your ears. A gray
heat swarmed your throat. *The briefest
face* you say *from cloud* you say. From the deep

north I watched & could
do nothing to help.

OURANOMANCY
divination by means of the heavens

Stasis equals your belief in a window. From it you see
a black maple spackle
a hospital's brick into aubergine. The glass carries a yellow
glaze of traffic, the whorl
of crimson wing tips, the slop
of salt-water. Up high in the elms, light
disappears into the bark of a bird that dips among the red
thrash of leaves. The voice of three

ships circle the harbor: where a small house
on the shore's made real by the sun. You would bury
your song, and walk backward keyless
into the sound of locks. That you were not
human. That there would be no one
to ask. But that you needed to
ask in order to live. Trucks

excite grasses under rain   bear scat   egg peel
of nut hatch   bird skulls
scattered through mulberry. There's
a ticking in the mind that thorns
and unfurls into thistle. You struggle still but can't
see what's missing. While

once you ask yourself why stumble. Ask yourself gentle
why laugh. You're not
special. You're not
not special. No comfort in language, real words
are soundless, but you gather no words, believing you still

hear him, but when you speak of his
voice you close the window to the ocean.

Radiesthesia
> *the science of using the vibrational fields of the human body to access information often using specially calibrated instruments*

His voice entered where it entered

Framing my isolation there   in between   the pointed oasis
as I call him back into the calm   into the too late

Oh please know—feeble I am in telling, as I go now with my assassin—the prairie
settles in my thumbnail as if a story could be scraped and traced back up
by meditation.   A child stranger arrives in my hand

as a circle of grass dispersed, molding
a small shave where the gauze of the old trees
broadly sluice the sky.
                      All this in my palm. Were I kissed
by the memorialization of snow I would slow
into immeasurable margins. By the rumor
you would not go back, I was made.

Were I the indecipherable names. My father
            in the analogous map of all fathers. His voice rose
     through the window. Now I like a stranger
hold my ear   pressed   incognizant,
uncareful. I was

intimate with his request that he might die. Since we were once walking together

beneath the interlaced spruce, fir, pine, since we were now walking into the near
spark   his short fibrillation
              and it is my third time back, under those needles

amid pots of geranium musk, as frankincense
warms the parameter.   Christen me by measures of dusk. Midnight,
part pantomime, is a blade

leveling metallic flames across the lawn.

Bequest

A blessing of ghost bees lulls the serum

of your speech. O, unlit fire. Your confection

in the mouth upon the mouth of whose name. Grass

in the whispered landscape leaks a dry glow.

Here primitive boughs of lilac

undress the swallow's eye. The bilious sky's

slow vigilance is re-born. And the quiet

of the fuck bodies, their infinite pages,

are laid open in the sun's library.

Belief

And I am turning the gold cache of the city's
outer rim, supplicating the surface with messages. I am with
horses. I am with deer. I am you with daylight. Though you cannot
see—

O languish—ghosts read the open hills,
                      the shadow's drunken length,
the cause and the effect of ghosts
in my voice where you are not answered. You might
come to me, acknowledged by endearment's offering. You might meet me
in the gloss, at the ravine's edge and we might call this
the lakeshore's equation
or the conspicuous midday blanche, or
                            the shimmering

Notes from the Blue Terrace

The pink lungs of a mule strain toward shade, his
yellowed lips saliva slick. The gardener wanders
late into the hills, unclothed in delirium. The nub
of his work thickens into bloom. He spends the day
threshing   thrashing   thatching until
the weight of a painted magpie
steadies him. One arm of the constellation
is a wing glazed with heat— a perfectly
beautiful waste of talent. Along the riverbank I water
my horse. The tin-rain-slosh shimmers
down her flank. The gardener stops and asks me:

What is it to die like this? He opens

his palm. He sees nothing in me astonished
by his offering. I am in the place he would not
circle—a lovely drop in his voice,
the makeshift sound of a tanager in the backyard
of a monastery. The gardener turns in shadow
to retrieve a blue trace of awkwardness. The sun
here is also crazed.

Ornithomancy
divination by observing flight of birds

The landscape: an inscription of dark pigeons   O, my beautiful one.

I dreamed your waking   I dreamed your eyes—

two boats drifting through a sea   with fire lining every shore.

The slow current records in cursive   the edge water: coil of foam and smoke.

More bright   grew the sky

        through which   all my papers and vespers

burned upward   as I traveled to find you.

So near is the sun you once loved.

        So blank and so peculiar.

The Guardian's Accurate Shotgun Upon Your Brow

Alone in the farm room you remained untouched
by the juniper rasp in the tree window. The funerary
rope from the mauled bodies hung from a north rafter. You
heard the chirrup of the kid-goat, the burned silverfish
in her fur lung. Too much energy to cry, so you
would. Holy apostolic field,
the doeling sloughs her radiance.

Now it is yours, stranger.

You held the mauled body, suckled
her sow eyes closed, undercurrent of lupine
in the mudbloom. You wanted to taste the clay
intestine, the corridor of her
far-off bells. Your Napoleon facade
beamed. Now it's

yesterday at the abbey, keyholes in limestone
revealed the missing
animal face. You kissed her
mildew knapsack, made a coat of minerals,
placed your body in the wood box, lit the stove. Restive

in your small purring, you consider

her nose capillaries leaking blossoms, what's left her
flees into the glade. Fascia of purple pollen
clouds the mountain, as does this guardian
who holds you her image as an accurate
shotgun upon your brow.

Dendromancy, Ex Nihilo Nihil Fit
divination by means of leaves and branches of oak

A lark-blue wakeling is the furnace's doctrine of visible richness. It is that
which I fear when the ceiling bears down. My mind's

withholding is motion alone

like the whole shadow of a blown star. I have reread my love
times and times, the purple tendering, a weird brilliance
beyond the driveway's flowering iris. I suppose

it's where the body's warmth is kept. At least
through the flare of one empire's duration. When the last border
of the soul was predicted, you arrived,

a child thing yourself, I asked you, out of whose dream
did your tiny god disperse, burning
your fortune's immensity? Might you
step outward whispering, *I saw you.* Might you name
the woods anew, stand in a thicket
among the unburnt pine
searching the distance granted
by your dominion. First you,
then you.

I have let home your dead. Let
snow loosen, glitter the earth.

In Release of The Coming Passage

In that dream there was a slow articulation of my absence. Deer
track through cedar, moss, and that long trespass, the wheel
I fall under into sleep. Nightly, my confidences spill

easily through the water meadow, the dead
arc through conversations, settling
into culverts awaiting the morning's
updraft. Fishhooks shine

off my sister's ear as we, here
in the hereafter, with our clay eyes, swim in the old
shifts of root. Restless

I move with my new
unanswerable mind—memory
is the motherly flavor of apple. Dear one,
I ask myself, with what language do
you dictate the violet wood shade I
once admired? Perhaps, I'll remain. If I

ever go back into that trance before
I began clearing the stairwell
of debris, clippings, old
snapshots and books, I might
salvage marked passages
I never returned to. Marginalia
guide me
           to what
crumbled between pages.

Catoptromancy
divination by mirrors

Unarmed, the woods possessed you.   Then against the songbird's throat
I pressed the lightest thorn. No path unearthed, except where
invisible wings soothed belittled air. Then you came in closer,
swarmed my sleep, trod the blue roots of unblessed crocus. Husks of snow
hid forgotten ships all over the hillside. Mainsails unfurled and love
anchored new blossoms. Then the flimsy threads of my coat
were your forest. I was not born out of earth's furrows
as that skinny schoolgirl. No, but of a beautified migration; ancestors
long procession found here in the basement of my lilac heart. Then,
near as a man I was smiling. I, the little lady of sublimations, a reindeer's tin eyes
at dusk among almond buds. Then balancing my coffee cup on the table's oval glass,
the sea's spark trapped my swig.   Then you would have seen me step
into the kitchen to light a cigarette, or dampen the heat
with a sip of ice. A little orchard of deaths
planted in exchange for want. Then between your hands
I could not undo desire. Oil slicks in the dark. Then circling
the others inside us. Reflections, I make you look by turning.

Moth, Horse, Accident, Skin

A moth's dull wings wetted into a brass crease. Once
someone remembered me

crossing the ravine. My bare feet stung on the sharp
cinder, rain slid the mudbank over which
orange blossoms sagged and the trill
echo of the last bird narrowed
the sky. Someone saw

me as I saw myself: a child scrawling
my name in the dirt with a rusted nail, straining
like the clang in the Elm tree
of a tiny bell, the wind was so faint
I could never wake
into it. All night, I lay
my chest over a stranger's back. My heartbeat
pressed his shoulder blade. I stroked
his hair as my hunger
stalled under the canopy
of summer heat, and the window filled

with a silent tick of snow. The muzzle
of a horse rose and lowered—once,
sharply. Following this, the original
shape of the mare reared
in flames. My pulse stung
my throat. I lay
trapped under the Cadillac's door as fire swept

the stubble field; smoke
like a crow's wing, flagged
the vetch and settled
over the old
date orchard, the sun
a blinding hallucination. I rubbed my swollen

belly's parchment of stretch marks. By noon, after weeding
I lay down in the yellow grass. The ache of labor
shines up through my shoulders, not wanting the inside
of my mouth to ripen, while two

moths gather under a street
lamp's green halo and drown
in a blossom of dusk.

Hyomancy
divination by the "tongue bone"

In the dark's lexicon of mosquitoes there was that other dark, a language pressuring the construction of nature. Messengers what was your message? The dream recorders plucked through piles of trash where rats and squirrels
rummaged beneath majestic shadow-rings of a lowing hawk. The circling in space is a great politic. As in past eras mice

ticked beyond snow's shell. Hundreds of clean antlers, the scrape of reindeer, hushed the printmaker's thumb. Believe words uttered the body. Hold your tongue, hold forth that lucent voice. Who speaks at the crossing when you were ready to cross.

The Arrival Memory

The soul inside the soul wants to talk.
It posts itself a letter. Close your eyes. You are a young man
riding a ferry over a frozen river
through a city that bears the soft
intention of steel. You
move among its cinder blocks and windows, and attempt

to rise—then a glistening fills
the channel. Stone wilts
under the current. Inland, suburbs spin
out of balance and sand plugs your throat. A voice that won't
drift keeps naming the water a blue afternoon. There is no
resolve. By spring, were you to ask

the June hyacinth of that windy note, the blossom's
long nights would be your first mercy. The moment

passes like a nerve in the wind, the velocity
of train. I'm kneeling. Something
I will never identify brushes upside my rib. Now

slit the envelope. Open it.

THUMOMANCY
divination by means of one's own soul

I would not notice your faint intrusion, but for the vignette edge
of the landscape, where your face
is an accident without origin.

I see you have been here all along. Let me tell you things
can happen in the years. Last winter a squirrel
died in the cabin
chimney. There is no

single script. Only the last three orders
of breath made before silence. Night has
given me my wide addiction. Under
uncertain laws, in the sleep of no choice, I follow
motivations downward into the sweep

of your pen. Scrawled lights of a new city
wink between rows of tamarisk. The center
of the book is a catastrophe, but
with love there is a lack

of distance. You have led me into the first
threshold of your vision. Jupiter
glows through a ragweed thicket. There is no
body. No sound. You go on without
calculation for the beginning. You go on

under the lowering
of gravity. Most

recent of animals, your lost papers fill
the closet. All afternoon you
constructed snow angels, turning your palms
skyward, but the gesture
of your hands were not holy. Tonight the oncoming
boxcar whistles your unfolding.

Epithalamium

But you remained that small girl who never looked up
as the nub of your yellow crayon
squared off a vacant paddock—beyond it a few perfect clouds,
a seagull's silhouette. So going,
you discovered a scribble of hair, a self-portrait, wind—caesura
of sleep. The steady darkness of the next room
caught in the doorframe. Through half open dream
a circle of crows flocked the verandah. As the night stilled its wing
His voice stirred—a radiant thrumming.
The flat moon divides the house with smoke. You sit at the hearth

choked with coughing until song breaks loose from the chimney
and a tremulous birdcall dismisses you. Tonight,
the rough slope of the hills reveal the bare shoulder
of a woman under the sky's changeless ink. For the first time
you see your beloved's eyes as two small rooms. Ragweed loosens

from your cinched hair as you kiss someone familiar. Later,
you will lie on the bed and stare at a diagonal
scar down the wall. If you gaze
long enough into this thin line you'll meet Him. He closes
His dim lantern
     over you   swiftly.

Alphitomancy
> *divination using barley cakes that are digestible by persons with a clear conscience but give indigestion to others*

Threadbare my lord, your sun connotes a soundless persuasion. Oddly earth-bound by indelicate oak limbs, the chalk fragment of leaves, burls blanched by winter's machinery, grief rises. Gently your words came.

Eventually a door opens, dreaming the omission
of water. It may have been the sea, a distant boat being the moment
the body was persuaded toward fraction. Home
broke its hold. I sat at the table

in the room you last stood. Night tilted the kitchen, thus the future

of my tiny self fell between the horizon's two-story brightness. I held my fingertips to your fingerprints, smeared on the sky's padlock, where a hive of transparent bees blew the curtains. Like the conflation of rain.

Under the hindrance of a linnet's kiss, a pleasant scratching cocks my ear. Love repeats the impression of laughter. Music as premonition, speech as theory's meter. All tenderness metes out. But you too are worn. A little heart-thump between stratospheres.

FUGITIVE

First I'll drink my rye
For there will be no one
but me & the house & the shade
ticking over the mountain

No one   need forgive me
my strange manners   my long dissent
toward floorboard   Even in the trembling

heat the afternoon won't kill
me   But the skin
breaks   & the skin
bears

When I press my finger into the glint
my name's a thickening smudge

Accidental Sea

The sea was not an accident
but a silk red dahlia hidden
in the curio-cabinet, a dusty
boutonniere which lurked under a shrunken
ship inside a bottle.

When T. said he loved me
every teacup in the house grew
stained & suffered a chip, the asphalt rippled
like some kind of water. It lashed
at the hedges. And I grew hungry. Desire teetered
in and out of the white-lit house like flies.

I measure myself against every
wreckage. The courtyard

flutters with light; the trees a dappled
crisis of wind. Past the glamorous town, birds
die off and by mid-summer a small vineyard
dries into thistle, moss, a stubble of weeds
and a mound of sand. No,

the sea was not an accident, but convolutions
in the rubble coursed against a heaving tide & the eyes
rimmed in drunkenness appeared larger, bluer.

Necromancy
divination by means of communication with the dead

Where all the deciduous trees break open and are washed out, at that place in Monroe, Iowa. When the waitress takes your order in that far away diner, you will blink. You consider the looseness of your thirst. You will be cut into the song of katydid. Occasionally a high beam touches your forehead. The silver jangle of beads grace your ears.

Lay down tonight under the tender weave of bells, flowering hazel, strange music. Thistles in your wool sweater. Later this fall you will know you were not alive. Essence of mushroom and scotch. Swarm of the three grouse. What finds you again is you. You who find love in secret will not know the tremble of the body. Your hair will be filled with kisses, larkspur, birdseed. A crown of bees fill the mirror.

Aureola

A rabbit lies buried under yellow cottonwood leaves
among a wet mulch of straw & dung.   Sawdust
drifts under streetlights. Dirt thickens the fingerprint
on the window ledge. You are tired
& close to sleep when your lover's name

stings your ear—the long dead
in the mind of the living.

Through the screen door
a swift's low chortle balances
the room's dizziness as a swarm of ants
brush over the crumbs of a raisin pie
& drips of stale coffee. Dawn

glazes the flank of a lame horse, what remains
of your house is an overgrown
apple orchard & a screeching
of birds. A breeze parts your eyelids

slightly; the black maple
taints your lips & brows
as the green of a stale wind swells,
with it, the scent of sycamore
& mothball. It's as if you'd traveled

all night through the marsh when
she rose out of the lagoon—water glistened
down her ribs, deerflies
gathered over her left areola.

PHYLLORHODOMANCY
> *divination by means of clapping a single rose leaf between one's hands*

No visible evening falls. Sweetness occurs from the first breath,
                              immediate and familiar. Snow
    west of the waterfront. Am I elsewhere. Capable
of missing the deer among the fir trees. Wandering
the imaginary body, they roam aglow. How
        do you remember the missing? I write toward
sand sifting clear into the mouth as the cactus wren
                in the town garden cull scorched thorns
for seed. The mind at this level can be poked. Pride
capitulates to beauty. My pleas obverse. Wild rose, I will
        go on all night beating sapphire into the sea.

SEAAMONG SEA

Tonight the confused waters
Still the sail, like the shifting
Rudder of my gaze, askance,
And respond: the young one gathers the rope,
Weeds caked in her hair. She drowned
Last summer.   The clean deck passes
Over her head.   Familiar
As a slip knot; her name   an Aegean-gold,
Anchorage deep in winter. Backward
Through the olive grove past the copper surface
Of the sea, a mixed purpling of veins
Or currents, beneath that granite arch,
She is buried.
                Remember dawn
Glowed upon her face—even here where the submerged
Cypress no longer pretend a windbreak. Catholic blue,
Saint blue—her eyes, slightly slighted
Pools. The last bottle of scotch
Dried while Sunday's papers
Splashed the wooden deck, sinking in fog . . .
Ask again
            from what glazed ship you might travel.
The sea lies dense and unread.

Cledonomancy, Sleep in the Raven's Throat
divination by means of chance remarks that are spoken without premeditation

Stitch by stitch in the shore's seam I measured fog's rotation. Thick loaves
of air rounded stone cliffs. Waves bit gulls in a loose crochet. As you plucked
a clear path of allegiance into your small environs, the lesser nighthawk
foraged under a streetlamp. Had you seen the faces of the holy?
Had you overthrown what lifted you? For hours
I'd mended the black pages of water and the creases
in the sand where you disappeared. From my sleep
in the raven's throat I saw you walking in the sun. I've forgotten
the depth of the lake. The liquor swill of reeds under your skin.

Absentia

Your breath is the sound of a rusted can
rattling from a string about to snap. Beneath
closed eyelids rimmed with gold you track
a bonfire's green wing, the shore edge
too far from a teetering
ship as it enters the glass waters
of a harbor. You will not wake
into the palm of the sea as waking is a thorn
pressed sharply to your breast; instead
listen for a garden. Flush to your ear: a buzzing
takes over, not cicadas,
not a band-saw, but a metallic ringing—
the complexion of death—a dirty bronze
like old money. You wander each room of the house

only to find an outpost where a mailbox
sinks in the marsh. The chirrup of an unseen creature
shifts through the dry grass. Love,
it is morning now. The last rib
of clean light. The air
a bruise we inhale. And so I will rise
under the dim unfurling dawn in the soft dark
to sip at the revision of a breaking sky—an illusion
of blue lakes flecked with spent stars.

Sciomancy
divination by means of communication with shades of the dead

The terebinth tree releases too late; moiré chemise spills through the boughs.
A goodwill coat closets the red serge, Swiss-dots, shade spurts in the silent palate
of owl moss. I saw my love walking in the field. He lay down among the Spinifex
and Spirea. Our post-coital vows trespass the private pines. Less hot the rain drones
among the spruce. I hear him. His tinseled leaves carpet his uncarpeted house.

Floromancy
divinations by means of flowers

Stammered currents rouse banks of purple crocus. Your birth occurred when

the pale afternoon waters hallowed a line of tamarisk trees. You now follow its spine of
dry needles. Had you made an error, then you might walk east, never noticing

the cow dung and the boots of a passing soldier lay against lucent birch. Back through
wood rot, you shiver in a blade of heat, an eel in your jugular, your voice,

a solar inflection can no longer carry your words. One would say
it might be over. But out of the sky's distillery of starlings another replies
that they will usher you. Your beard is a barnacle lowering the thirst of a dog's bark
into the green, beyond which barber boats and pontoons
drift like scores of unnamed mammals. You

are midnight, a black sun, roots washed, catching a thread of gnats off the surface
of the river. But your motions may be a meaningless addenda, a mixture of breath's
aperture, entrails, lobelia. You will not be greeted. Salvia

spirals up from a flickered bottle backed by a sputtering lantern. The doorway
is a stream upon which the lantern sets. Hunger

softens a spume of flies. Your infection blossoms.

Ensign March

The red splintered door, shade
of chokecherry, splits

the house into spheres.
You lie naked, less than sparrow, less
than cottonwood, and eye
a flickering moth. Outside, snow

strikes black limbs of oak; the sway
of branches twist eastward. Does it matter,
in this one season, who passes

or why. The steady hooves of a slow horse fill the arroyo
along with the sound of a slipping pack,
a few breathy groans. A sharpened

axe and stacked cordwood remain
neatly dry in all this falling. The rock salt
scattered over gravel beside the shed slops

the ground into a sheen. You draw a breath, a bath
and remember the dog tags in the desk drawer;
remember your body is somewhere
buried nameless.

The Widowhood of Charlotte Keese

The orchard flared orange at sunset. She looked up
from her stitching as the soldier crossed
the paddock to deliver the letter. Wind
tore at the windows. Her hair hung
like a black tangle of burrs
over her bare shoulder. Charlotte

pressed the scrawled envelope to her cheek
only to hear the sound of carnations
blooming, a clear sleep
under the cypress, the gate slamming open.

She wrapped the soldier's ankle
in clean linen doused with camphor. Thinned
down to sinew, the widow promised him
a seedbowl of turnips from the winter field. She was filled

by an unwilling language   most conscious
that she would touch him
and be found *ready to touch*. She loved him
without asking his name.

The ground this night was indigo.
Trees succumbing to the snow— branches
crippling. He liked hymns
and so she sang. Her passing body

remained the only ache.
Who is she now? She slept with it
over and over.

By spring a trail of daffodils uncoiling from frost led
her past granite hills. Sunlight syrup-thick
wet the late afternoon. She undressed

up to the hips. Even now
she feared the roots of his death
unfolding inside her. And above her
the sky gleamed bright without fault.

Spring

Bell through the long gate
rings a prayer. She speaks
into the clear metal above the trees
as dreams, strange wagers, wake spilling
like hands over the fields spilling
the curtains wide through a thin chaff
of light. The season's balance now
lost to him—the mad one, wind struck

and quiet. The sun remained unwritten,
but now the thin crush of its heat
is calm at the table along with the burnt
fragrance of bees. The door opens in wilderness,
framed in bayberry, where a diluted slow
swirl stirs the thaw, ending again the blare
of ice. Witnessing the lake's blind currents like faded

fingerprints on glass. She
remembers the beginning, lamplight
wetting asphalt streets, remembers touching
his throat's dappled grief
under hedgerow of juniper. His face
moth shadow, bowed into the flicker
of blue enamel, the warm
brevity of coffee, when
she snaps shut a locket over his hair.

BELOMANCY
divination by the flight of arrows in which three arrows would be marked with the phrases, 'God orders it me,' 'God forbids it me,' and the third remains blank.

1. God orders it me

    Was I words? Was I rib worn? No, I had simply died many times and been flung deep between dry ferns. My coincidences were laid out under the moon's weight. Nothing more was spoken. The doorman's marble eyes dared me. Constantly surprised by the luck of things, the weasel and the dove drove, sedative, amidst a rise of clouds. With me, I took my visage, my epitaph, imbued with the mark of this planet, the curt language of worms, the worn gleam of accident.

2. God forbids it me

    Mine essence flew the high feel of birds, the look of new trees and the peace found in their spring shoots and blossoms. Dragonfly, indeed, the nectar-like shine of your skin answers my spirit!

3.

    I will consult with your grief for free. I will watch your departing. The nostalgia of the pedestal you created for the lewdness of the world, your pining away for it! God, I will warm the obscure sixth lock, defrost the hock of lamb. I will follow out your shine when you walk boldly toward the solid door. Cruel declarations abound in the forgotten thickets, dotted with your name. Someone has given you a watch and called me to pile all your old bones in the cabinet. Oh king inside the mannequin, more twigs go projected into flotsam on the sea's surface.

    Which childhood do you remember? Oh, now we are getting somewhere.

Rhapsodomancy for an Imperfect Forecast
divination by opening works of poetry at random

Bibliographic pages spread a wind whipped trail
across our prior separation. Night advanced through aspen.

When was that love to become? O, wastrel, I believe you whispered of it at our last beginning just as we passed the first of those five gates. Clematis journeyed upward from the farmhouse chimney. The first gate opened while your mother's yard was cleared.[Gate 1]

So quickly came the trespass of hostas, little witch pilgrims, lining their wide-brimmed hats along the hedgerow. In the last encounter, camera grass fills the binding. You wait in this luminous circumstance with a fixed look of loveliness, motion gracious as a reed by Babylon[Gate 2] as my grief swells in the wide cottonwood leaves where you tune the yellow shade, brace the sun, teach me *I love you* in six languages. Your mother

dreams of walking backwards out in the world;[Gate 3] traveling has always
been easier for the dead. By the afternoon you said she must
be lonely.   *Yes* came coffee. *Yes*, I stroke
your hair. *Yes* you, emperor among the slowly human. You with women. Or you
alone. No matter. You pushed them all in one direction.[Gate 4] Wrappers
fill the streets, distant radio static
blares. After you left, your thought-form was
pokeweed, tarot card, sometimes *iris*.

[Gate 1] original quotation "while your neighbor's field is cleared..." by Arthur Sze, "After A New Moon," *Kenyon Review*, June 2010

[Gate 2] original quotation "Motions gracious as reeds by Babylon..." by Anne Spencer, "Lines to a Nasturtium (A Lover Muses)"

[Gate 3] original quotation "Now his mother dreams of walking out in the world..." by Joshua Weiner, "The Bed," *Threepenny Review*, Fall 2004

[Gate 4] original quotation "The flowers in this painting all are being pushed in one direction" Joan Colby, *Smartish Pace*.

Tá grá agam ort

Expansive, our habits grew more habitual. I wanted the wish for you to stay
to stay; I wanted that deeper than blood density. My broken
music bore your lip's sweet seam. Deities projected
through the bottle on your desk. Already you were trying
to touch their pleats, meeting the physical
instinct for home with longing. Even the coming train would not
wake the body. Guardrails moved alongside
your sleep, with its single mattress. I peeled myself
from the remaining protections, medallions' enamel-green Mary,
old amber prayer beads, language fabricated
out of coat threads mineral silence.

Aishiteru

You blushed as your fawn-rimmed eyes
observed the low movement of past suns. Regardless,
autumn's embodiment—bee's music blossomed
through us; vitreous
shade streamed artemisa, stargrass, wild leeks in that
last moment.

Szeretlek

Another night was given; that
trade in the mirror—you declared what
you were. Or
you wondered. So
little left to be needed. I wrote
into the woodlands until
I found you. Now there's a stream
across the sky's alphabet.

Te Amo

Your burial song makes me think
of vertigo, a chortle
of deathbirds. The thought of your slight
torso, that palpitation
of lilies, the pain in the back
of your memory: your death

before your death. Heat's capacity for
maggots moistening the gold
after-effect. So absolute is grief's circumstance, it whispers I
love you just as its love curses
the body. I knelt before the small black
and white plane of your face, its faded
meadowlands where a flowering
ghost-weed addresses
the rain. Your three
fingers unfold, pressing your lips.

Je t'aime

Upsidedown night, between water insoluble
cloud, your breathing signals held
sway with the willow. Slow spells came. The slow
spread beneath the skull.

Nu' umi unangwa'ta

The Hopi believe the cottonwood leaves quaking are the gods speaking.

Oromancy While Waiting for the Beloved
divination by means of observing mountain shapes

My beloved wept touching the firm neck of his horse. The plains of his
compass met in the low grass at a spot
where a line of smoke trees receded. An inconstant murmur

held his palm across the horse's mane
as a metabolic crosshatch rose in the lungs—a smoothness, like wind,
but without sorrow in the breath's dirt dark throb. My love

traveled by horseback on one of the last twelve roads known
to pass through the river into the north gorge. We'd

come from the same wound in the clearing. Perhaps

it was the end of marriage, the transmutation of leaves
shivering upright, or snow broken into
a million waters.

Sambucus Road

I might stress that the French blue lanterns passing through each window
were like goals set high enough to underscore defeat. In the backseat
we piled carriage blankets up to our hips.

Northward, Manzanita brush burned with lion-color deer. Your hunger
filled me, but would not be sated. This slurry of nectar gleamed, succor in the
quake of your palm.

We were kept quiet. The warm hay of winter spread
over the last road, and a tender tropic awakening the labor, those honeycomb
chambers, the leaf lobed heart.

Swallow's morning chorus, copulation. We listen. *Suéltame. Suéltame. Ven.*

Ilex Road

We drank behind the barn
which came with it's own sky.
We drank until elegies bore pattern.
You turned your eyes into the furze
or maybe it was milkweed.

Alnus Road

A variable tumescent held the gate open to a plasticized universe without petticoats. Anger parched reflections upon cigar box. Named after gunpowder. My horse-tongue ruby. O, my horse-tongue.

Salix Lucida Road

Cratae Road

Quercus Road

Betula Road

A small green patch in the gravel where our lady of moss now gives

brodieas an auric scar. O, forgive us. We don't mourn the loss of water deep enough to be medicinal—

The seer hides in steeplebush, casts us into sparrow stasis. Until we are banished by yarrow's yellow umbel. We wanted

Aucupari

to go back to the dominion of angels.
We each mapped etiquette's extremes,
then went forward uncensored.

Without you

there was that other place. The soul craved

it's crawlspace traced with lavender.

Fraxinus

Hamamelis Road

Muriel followed my grandmother
from hill to hill, spitting wide her amethyst hair.

Calcium emptied all through cornfields. Her seersucker dress
stopped among calculated rows of pigeonweed. I wanted to kiss her.

Hedera Road

The horse returned. Miasma between doorways, time

beyond the sun. This wasn't the first god. Just as, in the century's last pages,
night herons returned, milk oiled, dusted in the cinnamon surface of seed. Consider
here the deity who marveled. The one

who traveled through mirrors to capture
the size of death, the curve of it inside the physical
fear of men. *John,*
she'd say, *the body is coming.* All

through the house sibyls chattered—given
reason to translate birdsong so that you might recognize her voice within
the mimicry of church bells,

her syntax, that rusted key
Ziplocked in saltjar, would open the sonnet, but you
were lawless. Without convention, you reminded
her of heaven. This

is where you started. Where you felt it. Most days it was so

simple to love, and to give everything but—
neon vacancy signs, pools
of candy-light, inlets of roadside motels, like a hidden
curiosity for the obsolete—love.

Arundo Road

Out of season Verchiel fed us green garlic soup. Witch tonic. Vestige
of red admiral moths stirred the filigree patterns of burl. Salvia stars I might
write to under truce. Under weed-tree. Opposite
of a stranger, but still strange; I wrote

into the dark, declaiming over
overgrazed spirals, the animus
of the clearing. My raven

skin shone under the luck of my ringed hair. Clock slow. Nightgown's
silk phrase laced my shoulder. The bones
of the river evacuated the snow. It wasn't so
long ago.

Eromancy
divination by means of the air

O inevitable architect, in your false prime the last of your images blew off in a breeze of sawdust & chalk. At the fair, I stole a pinhole photograph of the moon. I carried apple blossoms floating over a black lake in my coat pocket. Your name, I ingested. Now light empties over waves imitating driftwood, a dry weight, counterbalance to what love abandons. The thought of blood in my arteries remains an illogic warmth. I remember the earnest, but now uncertain, affections. The night tilts. Silver tokens, perhaps stars. I stand among the living reading your initials. White ink tattooed on water.

Spring Tattoo

There is a Xeroxed orchid in the snow deep garden
that does not waver   even as worm-yellow birds,
thick as chenille, tear at its stalk. Your chest sunk

in the ochre glare as a mute tumble of afterthought
spread outward into the thick
grasses beyond the town's cubicle.   I listened to you

though you were already dead.   Bobby pins
clipped a dragonfly to your hair. Gentle to the self

in the way of speech, was I in my invulnerable
suit of appearance, like a bearsuit—flameproof & grizzled
with the stench of old sweat & other lovers—sun glint
as history. I am what guards you now

by waking you inside my flat stretch
of mind that will not pass.   And my gray-gravel
wall you will blow against. Constraint, seasons

I have asked you in

in the shade white & blind.

What circular lie have I loved,
with full lips of commitment. When no one said

they would ever have me. Inmates
beautify the I-95 roadway stepping twice
to expose tread-prints on an illuminated sheaf.

Ostentaria
divination based on the direction from which certain birds call

Saint of the small heart's skull, in half-presence, what
questions you? You leave, are buried, and thrown back
into back-story. Do you rest again among lanterns
with your two brothers? You cannot kill the last sleep, nor
remain sole witness. Your marled words
stalk the waves of your breaking and are a kind of crawling. Your call rises
above lapwing gloom. Star Emissary, traveler of the last world. Your song's
                      a crooked weave, winter's near shine. But where
do the omen birds gather? I in my falcon skin, you
                                      up from marsh roots, stir
the mind's to-and-fro in a forgotten articulate: music, a bow's abyss. Dusk violins.
I'd just named the animal days an unsteady truth
as harriers pipe hollow psalms, and love, queried our will, a lost language trembled.

Macharomancy
divination by swords, daggers and knives

A long slow gallop phrases your speed. You tarry slowly the horse through this race in which you never existed. That race of millions. There is one brightness in you which continues outside of you. One brightness, nameless, goes on thinking: *no, not you*. It is one brightness in a different picture that goes on, knife-like, bothering the impression of your body, carving its silhouette, sharpening the lone moment when god is strange and his haunting becomes a direction, like a series of yellow daggers on a map. O night of the sinewy mistress! Objects are set forth before you: feathers broken, mirrors of bird flight stream upon you. A string of hotel rooms, little sun hives. Shade flowerings of cotton sheets. Along the highway you yourself go walking, as if toward a known place. As if the little killings of that place are vacant without you.

Hanael's Mandala of Water, Grass, Sun

I guess I'd been preparing you to leave in
the way I was accustomed. Before
your sleep, thistle whipped the tides, and I was guided against shy

blossoms, barely tallied, toward that Ohio light. Taking in that
famous necrology of springtime impression, I lingered across those grasses dull
brown tongues of the dead you kept in mind. I paused
on the dissatisfied grey where reedy
lilacs broke into delicious spears. A bouquet of egrets

passed through cedar. Hurrying their slightness against the bank
of a transparent lake. Ridgeline,

no matter what your course, murmurous
warble under the luster of the sun's
damp cover will follow.

Magastromancy
divination of the future through astrological calculations and speculations

Mathematically wrong, the constellations were weakened by new probabilities
held in the blooming of elm, in phlox petals. You read the cues
as you walked through the house. The sun's equation is the moment
a stone becomes visible under water. These are not patterns held by dreamers
that vanish after dreams.

                                        Scrim of oil on glass, these are visions
addressed the moment your fingertips no longer restrain inchoate map lines. You press
your lips onto stone, onto water, onto grass.

Your hands are   an algebraic falling

full of augends and remainders.

You love the body. You love the middle of a sheer cloud.

If when I am attached and calculated from the otherside, death being a kind of fifty
percent belief system, like a letter you might open, tearing through though the envelope as
        an act of understanding. You wrote your own sky beyond the meadow
closed the light   wrote a new twilight.
    Stranger, let the shine move about.
    I believe the horse is my equation. I am to ride a thing called horse.

I am to ride beyond salt lakes at the empire's boundary. Snow drifts under lanterns. Spine
white strands. I put your mind into the hand of my other hand's heart. Guided by the
voices dwelling in other voices. One mind placed into another. A woman in the mirror
turns her back to the mirror.

Sideromancy
divination by burning straw on hot iron

Among the glass trees, specific are the smoke rings, their pale shadows flood an imagined garden. They whisper *I am necessary to exist. I am battled and survived by honeysuckle.* I have attempted to dissolve in singular fire-strikes the familiar arrival of moths. It is a strange chance, the turning moment of cold. *I am panic enough alive to be the wrecked one's heart.*

Apantomancy
divination through observing objects that appear haphazardly

Dear sun,

I settle into the your little cobalt landscape in the hills as the dead
are announced into a new universe.   Is this your payment, my aloneness? Lover,

when you beat my window there is no greater beauty I can think of. Asteroids, seeds,

tilt one direction only. The perpetual horizon is a calm impression
of your hands opening to me. In the bleating dark, your secret wife,
the moon's blue trajectory, wanders the roadside. Come lost winter one, souls
assemble in the cardinal's trees. Faith is a found philosophy, a ladder
flung across three freeway lanes. Along the internal corridor of grass
infantile sprigs of silver holly spread.   You finger my hair into garlands.
I am part of you without evidence.

Dear etiquette of slick lament,

I no longer recall the vocabularies of the disappeared. What is done is discounted
through every field: light bulbs among a mattress of daisies.

A floral upholstery chair blossoms under snow.

Enoptromancy
divination by means of using a shiny surface placed in water to foretell the recovery or death of someone

At dusk, moth laced diction, bees
                     articulate apple's aftermath. At the feast, I set a place for you among the dead. Cold stars languish under my crane skin dress. Sleep, snow's mechanism held in residue at midline.
                     Thou eyes old thirst lowers at last.

*

You tell me a woman stands ultraviolet among the rhododendron. You tell me two times the water. Three times sun. You tell me Le Conte's sparrow does not attack the larva of a tussock moth. Vicissitudes white daises aflame her brown streak breasts divide the mirror.

*

At the frost altar, before the afternoon slips behind the suburbs my cold terrible body like paper is delicately glazed, breakable. I was rereading of a woman's death in the snow... I was no expert on perfection, but I attempted it by studying a photograph of her body's small shape, a dark room against the wide white scale of the hill. And in my obsession I observed a crowd of mice lying dead just inside the door of her winter cabin. Mice, because of their ability to burrow into the ground, are believed by Baule diviners to be close to the powers of ancestral spirits below the earth's surface. The Baule believe mice could once talk. I wondered, even some months after, if perk ever returns. Even after death, the mice seemed to be smiling.

Frost Altar

Love blunted your song as heavy steeds to heels. Eventually, angels
at equinox, covenants arrived knowing the old question. But for the whole

of that one century a single crane's speculation yellowed me. Circuitous
his glance bore the cause that thickened the surrounding waters

into lacy white. There was no desperation in you who stood amid the awkward green—
where orchids leaked blackness, honing summer's petition unpersuaded, as when

I paced your small hospice room one last time. And the forest
tightened against blue wings, the windows shuddering with snow's fresh cut.

Notes

fuck bodies, see "sun's library"

Hanael's Mandala, *"Water-Grass-Sun"* from *Rigveda Mandala 1, HYMN CXCI*

"I love you" in six languages: *Tá grá agam ort* (Gaelic), *Aishiteru* (Japanese), *Szeretlek* (Hungarian), *Te Amo* (Latin), *Je t'aime* (French), *Nu' umi unangwa'ta* (Hopi)

"Oromancy," the last twelve roads are based on the scientific names for trees

Suéltame. Suéltame. Ven. (Spanish) translates as, "Let me go. Let me go. Come back."

sun's library, see "infinite pages"